NATURE WORDS

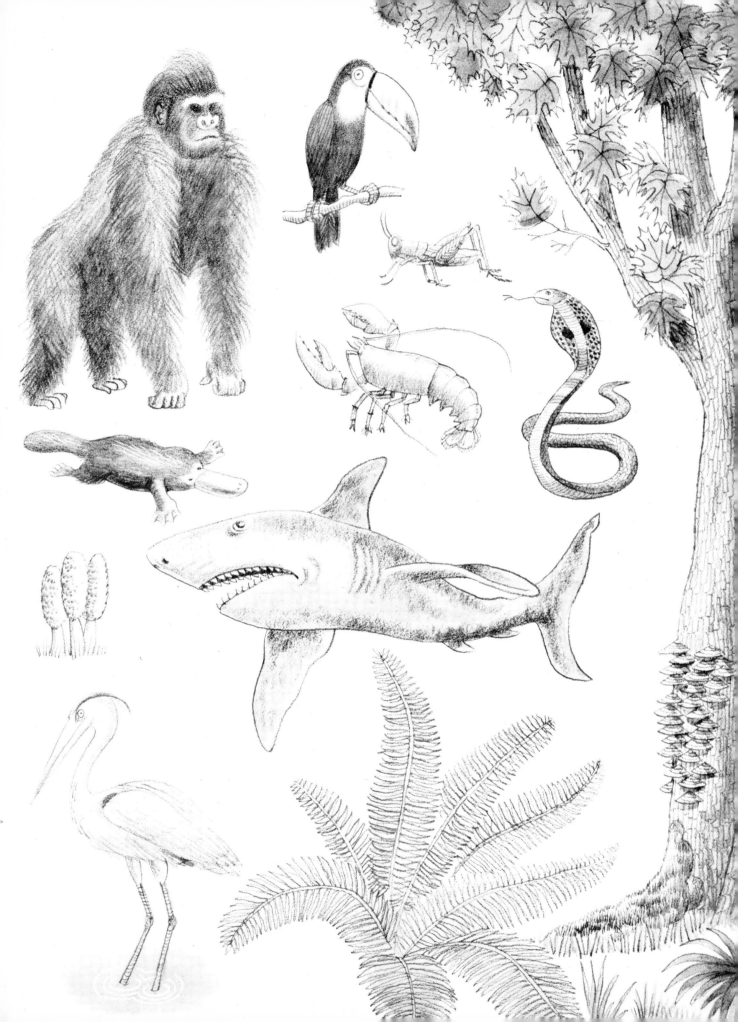

To Bryna and Louis Untermeyer,
friends and lovers — of words
and of nature

BIRD

LEAF

BRANCH

TWIG

INSECT

MAMMAL

BARK

REPTILE

AMPHIBIAN

ARACHNID

FUNGI

FISH

BIRD

CRUSTACEAN

RODENT

FLOWERS

NATURE WORDS

By KATHLEEN N. DALY

Illustrations by ROBERT PIERCE

Over 1,000 bird words, fish words, snake words, spider words — all kinds of plant and animal words with pictures, glossary, and index

Publishers · GROSSET & DUNLAP · New York
A FILMWAYS COMPANY

ABOUT THIS BOOK

Children are becoming interested in nature at a much earlier age these days. Even toddlers are avid admirers of flowers and animals. Children also like to study nature books. But these books often presuppose a knowledge of fairly technical words, such as *antenna, seed, spore, larva.* And dictionaries can be intimidating, not only to the young, but to their parents. This first book of "Nature Words" is an attempt to explain, in simple, unsophisticated words and pictures many of the terms that will confront the young nature lover in his first explorations of the world around him.

At the back of the book is a Glossary-Index, which not only helps in looking things up, but further defines hundreds of useful words.

For the author and the artist this book was a labor of enthusiastic learning. We hope that some of it will rub off on the reader, and send him on his way to discovering more about the wonders of nature.

Text copyright © 1976 by Kathleen N. Daly
Illustrations copyright © 1976 by Harper and Pierce, Inc.
All rights reserved
Published simultaneously in Canada
Printed in the United States of America
Library of Congress Catalog Card Number: 74-17720
ISBN: 0-448-11914-5 (Trade Edition)
ISBN: 0-448-13248-6 (Library Edition)

Contents

DAISIES

STRAWBERRIES

MAPLE TREE

APPLES

WHEAT

SEAWEED

REDWOOD TREES

CELERY

TULIPS

MUSHROOMS

ONIONS

CARROTS

CATTAILS

PALM TREES

MOSS AND LICHEN

GRAPES

Plants

It is lucky for us that the whole earth is covered with plants. Without plants, we couldn't live. There would be no animals on the earth, nor fish in the sea, nor birds in the air.

What is a **plant?** It is a living thing that can make its own food from **air, sunshine,** and **water.** Animals cannot make their own food. They must have plants to eat.

CACTI

CORN

FERNS

Plants
FLOWERS

A **flower** is the prettiest part of a plant. Because a flower has pretty **petals** and smells so good, bees and other insects come to visit it. They drink its **nectar,** or juice, and gather its **pollen.** The pollen may then be brushed off onto another part of the plant, or onto another plant of the same kind.

When pollen lands in the right place it travels down to the flower's seed-making cup or **ovary.** The pollen joins with tiny eggs called **ovules,** and new seeds are made.

THE SEED-MAKING PARTS OF A FLOWER

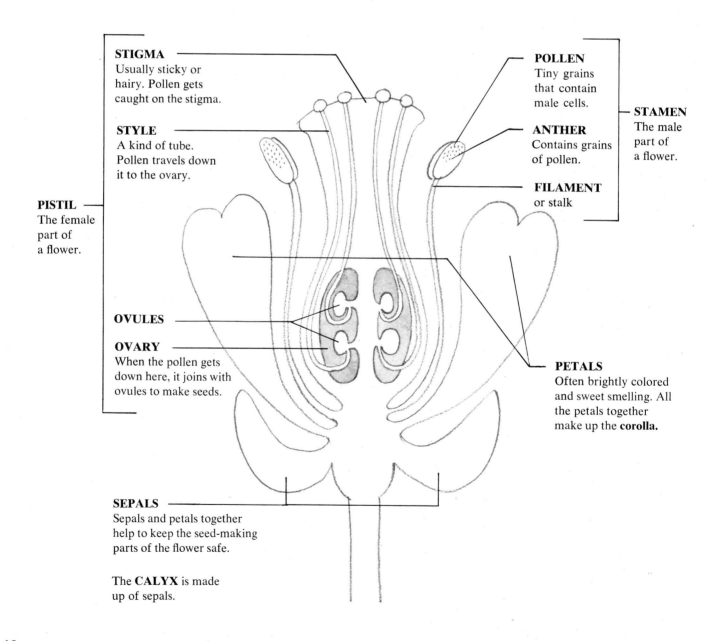

STIGMA
Usually sticky or hairy. Pollen gets caught on the stigma.

STYLE
A kind of tube. Pollen travels down it to the ovary.

POLLEN
Tiny grains that contain male cells.

ANTHER
Contains grains of pollen.

STAMEN
The male part of a flower.

FILAMENT
or stalk

PISTIL
The female part of a flower.

OVULES

OVARY
When the pollen gets down here, it joins with ovules to make seeds.

PETALS
Often brightly colored and sweet smelling. All the petals together make up the **corolla.**

SEPALS
Sepals and petals together help to keep the seed-making parts of the flower safe.

The **CALYX** is made up of sepals.

10

SEEDS

A **seed** is a wonderful thing. Inside it is a tiny baby plant. There is also food for the new plant. Sometimes there is food all around the outside of a seed, too.

PARTS OF A SEED

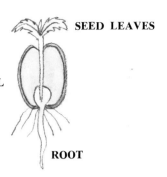

SEED LEAVES

SEED SHELL

ROOT

These fruits contain seeds:

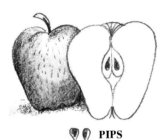

PIPS

APPLE

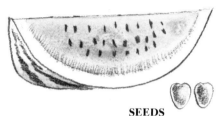

SEEDS

WATERMELON

PEAS in a pod

SEED

COCONUT

Seeds travel in many ways:

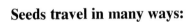

BY WATER (Water Lily)

BY AIR (Dandelion)

CHERRY

With the help of ANIMALS

How seeds grow

When the seed finds a warm, damp, safe pace, its coat, or shell, breaks open. A tiny **root** comes out and pushes its way into the earth. At the same time, the little **seed leaves** push upward toward the sun. A new plant starts growing.

Some roots go deep underground. Some spread out for many miles. They send **water** and **mineral foods** to the plant. They help keep the plant steady so it won't blow down in the wind.

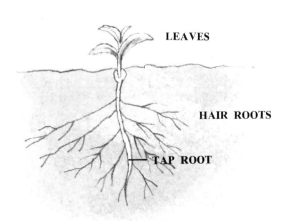

LEAVES

HAIR ROOTS

TAP ROOT

11

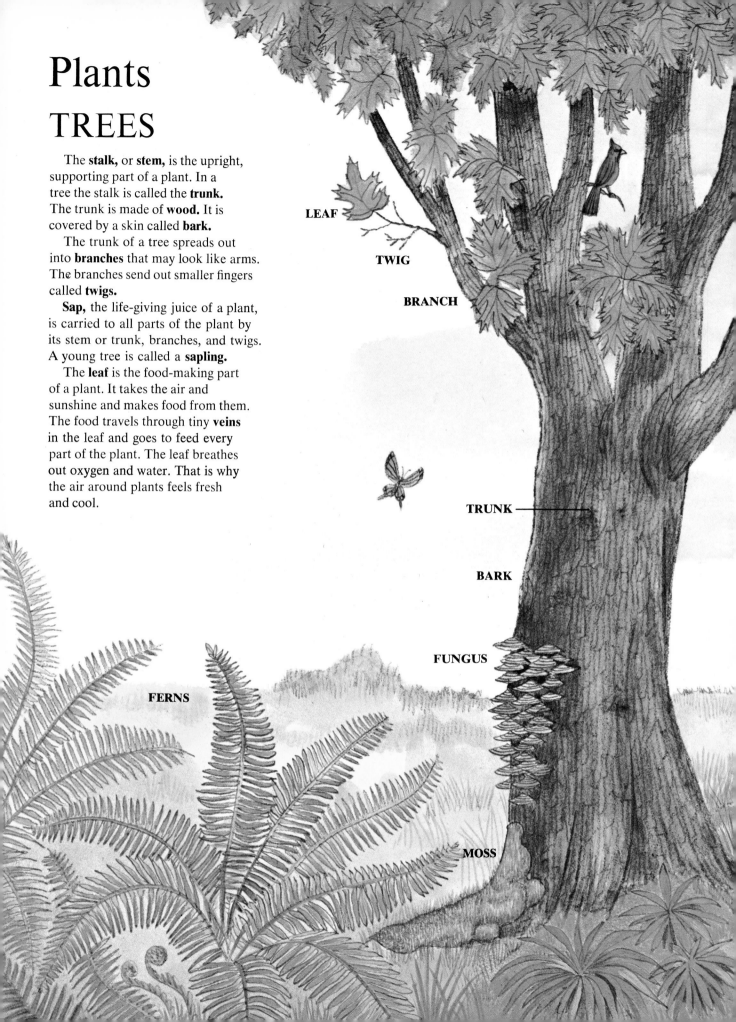

Plants
TREES

The **stalk,** or **stem,** is the upright, supporting part of a plant. In a tree the stalk is called the **trunk.** The trunk is made of **wood.** It is covered by a skin called **bark.**

The trunk of a tree spreads out into **branches** that may look like arms. The branches send out smaller fingers called **twigs.**

Sap, the life-giving juice of a plant, is carried to all parts of the plant by its stem or trunk, branches, and twigs. A young tree is called a **sapling.**

The **leaf** is the food-making part of a plant. It takes the air and sunshine and makes food from them. The food travels through tiny **veins** in the leaf and goes to feed every part of the plant. The leaf breathes out oxygen and water. That is why the air around plants feels fresh and cool.

LEAF

TWIG

BRANCH

TRUNK

BARK

FUNGUS

FERNS

MOSS

SPORES

What is the difference between a spore and a seed?

Most plants that we see started out as seeds, which come from flowers. Even the biggest trees start life as seeds. But there are many other plants that come from **spores.**

Both seeds and spores help to make new plants, grow. But a **spore** is tiny and delicate. Its walls are very thin. It must find a place to grow as quickly as possible, or it will dry up and die.

A **seed** has a sturdy covering or **shell.** Inside the shell is enough stored food (formed by seed leaves, or **cotyledons**) so that the new plant can live easily until it begins to make its own food. A seed can rest for many months, or even years, until it finds just the right place to grow.

ALGAE

An unopened leaf or flower is a **BUD.**

MUSHROOMS

Plants

ALGAE

Some of the plants that grow from spores are so minute that we can't see them except under a **microscope.** There are millions of microscopic plants all around us — and inside us! Many of them belong to a big family called **algae.**

The **scum** you see on a pond is a kind of alga. So are the **seaweeds** that you find on the beach. Seaweeds grow deep in the ocean or along the shoreline and often get swept ashore by wind and waves. Many tiny algae live in the sea, where fish and other sea creatures feed on them.

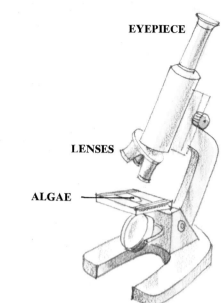

EYEPIECE

LENSES

ALGAE

MICROSCOPE
The **lens** helps make things bigger so we can see them.

SEAWEED

FUNGI

Mushrooms or **toadstools** belong to another big plant family called **fungi.** **Mold** and **mildew** growing on stale bread, or cheese, or on books and leather, are fungi, too.

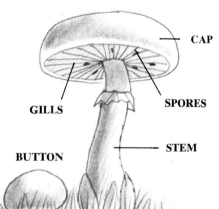

CAP

GILLS

SPORES

BUTTON

STEM

SHAGGY MANE MUSHROOM

DESTROYING ANGEL
(poisonous)

STINKHORN

LICHENS

The dried-up, gray-green plant on the side of this rock is a **lichen.** Lichens are really two tiny plants, an alga and a fungus, that always live together as one plant.

LICHEN

MOSS AND FERNS

Little **moss** plants may grow so close together that they look like a soft green carpet on a stone or on the woodland floor.

Ferns like damp, shady places. Their leaves are called **fronds.** On the underside of their leaves you may find tiny brown spots. These are **spore cases.**

All of these plants, algae, fungi, lichens, mosses, and ferns, grow from spores instead of from seeds. They are **non-flowering** plants.

MOSS

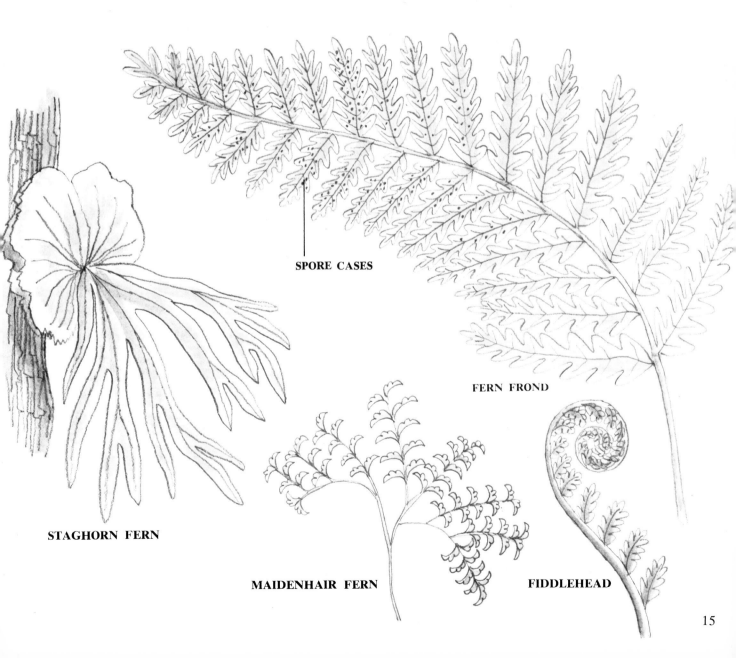

SPORE CASES

FERN FROND

STAGHORN FERN

MAIDENHAIR FERN

FIDDLEHEAD

Animals (Invertebrates)

An **animal** is a living creature that can move about. (A plant is living, too, but it can't move about.)

There are many thousands of animals in the world. Those animals that do not have **backbones** are called **invertebrates.** Many invertebrates live on the sea floor and look like plants. Only when they are first born do they swim about as little creatures called **larvae.** Soon they find a place to settle down, and there they stay, moving very little.

LIFE IN A CORAL REEF

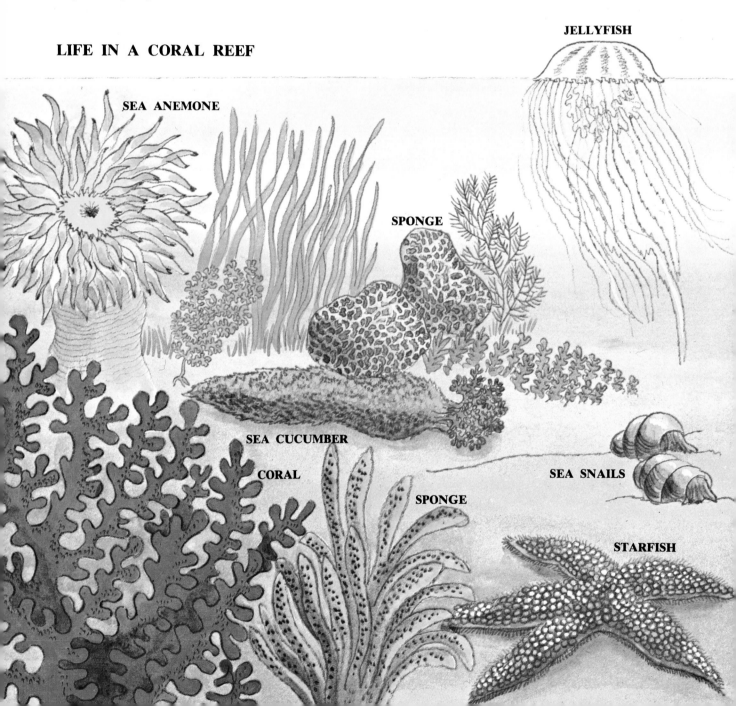

JELLYFISH

SEA ANEMONE

SPONGE

SEA CUCUMBER

CORAL

SPONGE

SEA SNAILS

STARFISH

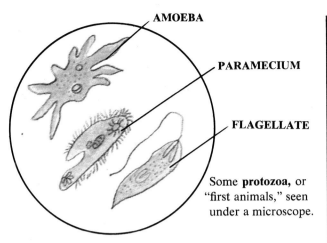

AMOEBA

PARAMECIUM

FLAGELLATE

Some **protozoa,** or "first animals," seen under a microscope.

Some creatures are so small they can be seen only through a microscope. They might have only one or two **cells** instead of the thousands that bigger animals have.

MOLLUSKS

The **mollusks** are a big family of invertebrates. Most of them have soft bodies covered with **shells.** Many of the shells that you find at the seashore belonged to mollusks. They are of all kinds of beautiful colors, shapes, and sizes. Many of them contain creatures that are good to eat.

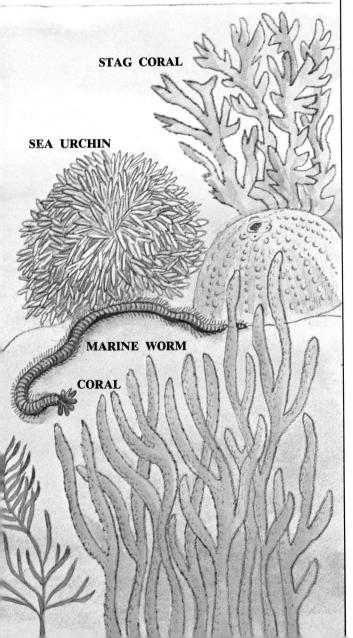

STAG CORAL

SEA URCHIN

MARINE WORM

CORAL

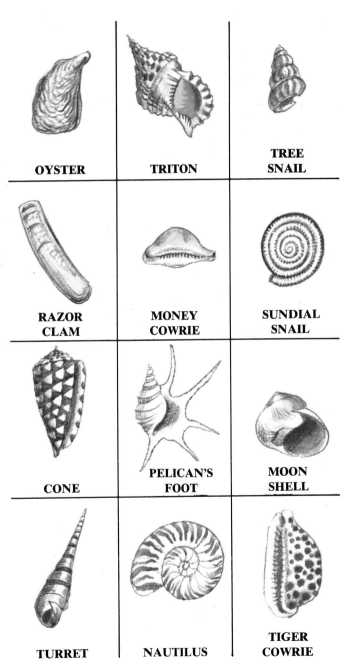

OYSTER	TRITON	TREE SNAIL
RAZOR CLAM	MONEY COWRIE	SUNDIAL SNAIL
CONE	PELICAN'S FOOT	MOON SHELL
TURRET	NAUTILUS	TIGER COWRIE

MOLLUSKS

SNAILS are **univalve** mollusks. Univalves are soft-bodied animals having only one shell.

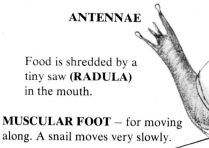

EYES

ANTENNAE

SNAIL

Food is shredded by a tiny saw **(RADULA)** in the mouth.

SPIRAL SHELL
The snail pulls its soft body inside its shell for protection.

MUSCULAR FOOT — for moving along. A snail moves very slowly.

SUCTION CUPS — for holding on.

SNAIL TRAIL — a kind of shiny carpet laid down by the snail so it can travel over rough ground.

OTHER UNIVALVES:

CONCH	**PERIWINKLE**	**WHELK**

ABALONE	**LIMPET**

The **octopus, nautilus, squid,** and **cuttlefish** belong to a mollusk group called **cephalopods,** a word that means "head and feet." Unlike the other mollusks, they move about a lot.

OYSTERS have two shells, or valves, hinged together. When a piece of grit gets inside its shell, the oyster covers the grit with smooth layers of **mother-of-pearl.** A precious **pearl** is formed. Mollusks with two shells are called **bivalves.**

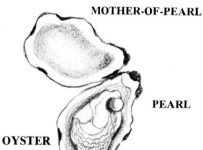

MOTHER-OF-PEARL

PEARL

OYSTER

HEAD

EYE

INK SAC

OTHER BIVALVES:

SCALLOP	**CLAM**

MUSSEL	**JINGLE SHELL**

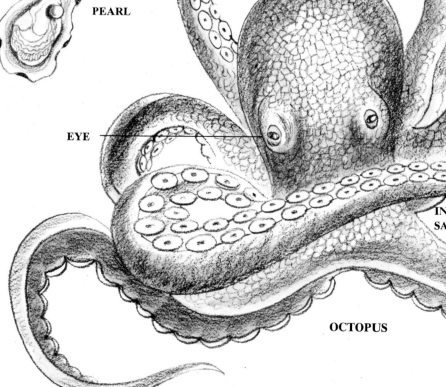

OCTOPUS

18

CRUSTACEANS

Shrimps, lobsters, and crabs are **crustaceans.** They live in the water on the sea floor. Their bodies are **segmented** and covered with a shell, or **carapace.** Their **antennae,** or feelers, help them to know what is going on around them. They have **pincers** (large claws).

The male fiddler crab has one claw much bigger than the other. You may see him waving it back and forth to attract a female crab to his burrow. Crabs often leave the water and can be seen scuttling about on the shore.

Hermit crabs don't have shells of their own. They live in old, unused shells, such as that left by a sea snail.

The horseshoe crab is neither a crab nor a crustacean. On the family tree of animals it is somewhere between crustaceans and spiders.

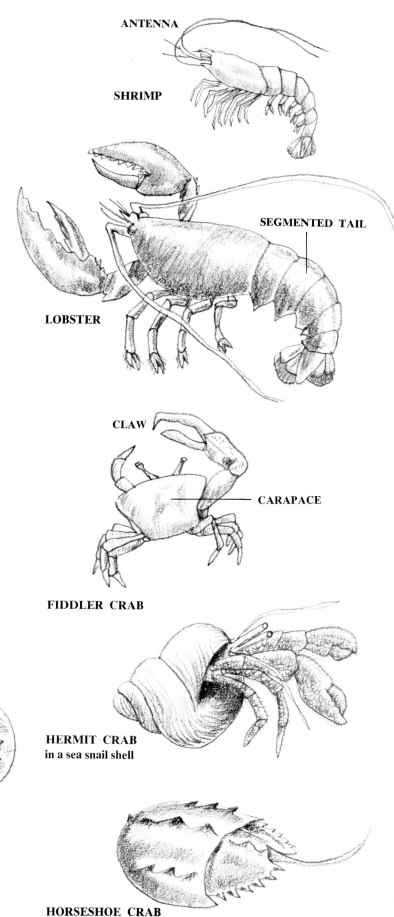

ANTENNA

SHRIMP

SEGMENTED TAIL

LOBSTER

CLAW

CARAPACE

FIDDLER CRAB

HERMIT CRAB
in a sea snail shell

HORSESHOE CRAB

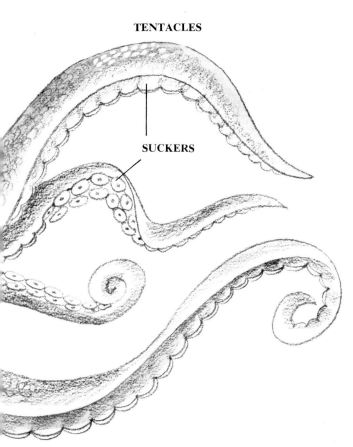

TENTACLES

SUCKERS

SPIDERS
and other arachnids

Many people think of spiders as insects, but they are not. Spiders have eight legs; insects have six. Spiders don't have wings; most insects do. Spiders have no antennae; they have feelers called **palps** or **pedipalps.** Their bodies are divided into two parts, (head and abdomen), not three.

WEB

INSECT PREY

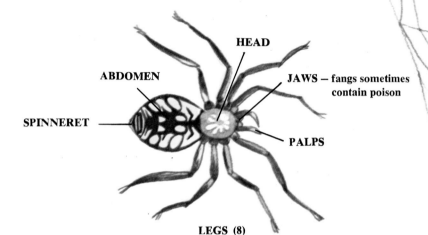

SPINNERET

ABDOMEN

HEAD

JAWS — fangs sometimes contain poison

PALPS

LEGS (8)

BLACK WIDOW

DADDY LONGLEGS

Spiders make "silk" from a liquid inside their bodies. The silk comes out through the **spinneret.** This silk, or **gossamer,** can act as a bridge, or a ladder, or a parachute (especially for baby spiders), or a **cocoon.** But most often it is used to make a **web.** Insects get caught on the sticky threads and the spider eats them. Spiders help keep our houses and gardens free of insects. Daddy longlegs (or harvestmen) and scorpions belong to the same class (**Arachnid**) as spiders.

TARANTULA

SCORPION

INSECTS

Insects come in all shapes and sizes.
They are very different from each other.
A fly is an insect; so is a butterfly.
A ladybird is an insect; so is a walking
stick. A mosquito is an insect; so is
a dragonfly. **Bugs** and **beetles** are insects.
Some people call all insects "bugs."
Bugs are only one kind of insect.
Beetles are another kind of insect.

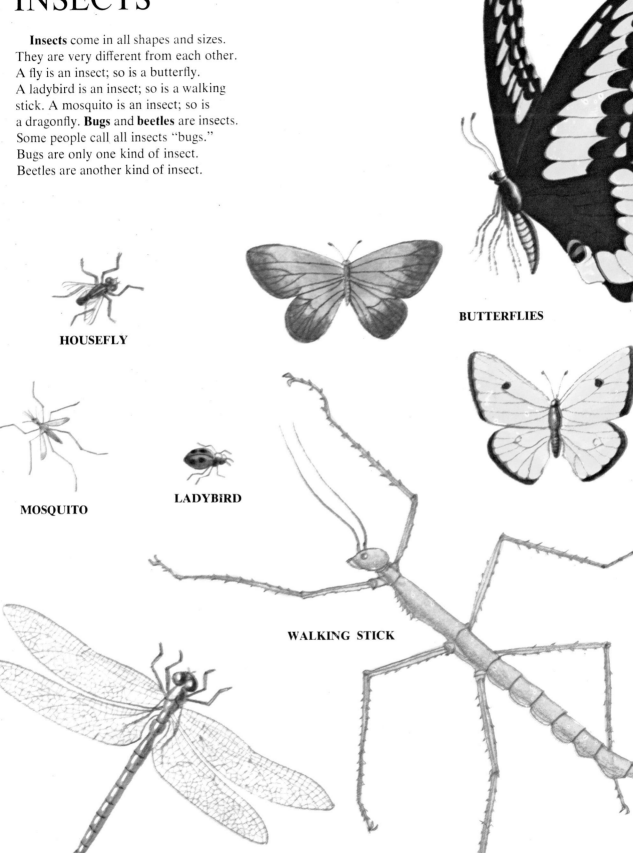

BUTTERFLIES

HOUSEFLY

MOSQUITO

LADYBİRD

WALKING STICK

DRAGONFLY

INSECTS

All insects have **six legs** and two **feelers,** or **antennae.** They may have one or two pairs of **wings.** Their bodies are divided into three parts: **head, thorax,** and **abdomen.** An insect may have **simple eyes** or **compound eyes,** or both, but it cannot see very clearly.

Its antennae, which are very sensitive feelers, help it to know what is going on around it.

An insect's **mouth** may have a hard **beak** for piercing and sucking. It may have strong jaws, or **mandibles,** for seizing and chewing.

Attached to the thorax are six legs and, usually, one or two pairs of wings.

The abdomen may have a **sting** at the end of it. Some insects defend themselves by stinging their enemies.

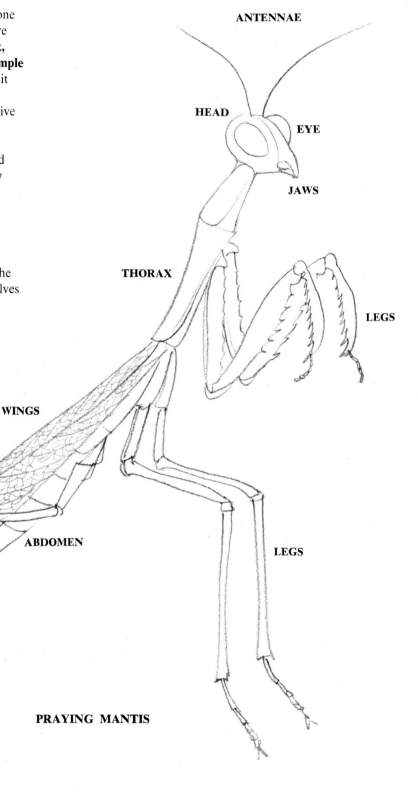

ANTENNAE

HEAD

EYE

JAWS

THORAX

LEGS

WINGS

ABDOMEN

LEGS

LEGS

PRAYING MANTIS

The jointed legs are used for:

HOPPING (Grasshopper)

DIVING (Diving beetle)

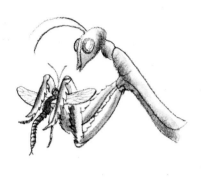

SEIZING PREY (Praying mantis)

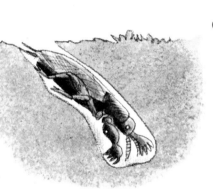

DIGGING (Mole cricket)

GATHERING FOOD (Honeybee)

CLINGING (Louse)
(Enlarged)

WALKING (Ant)
(Enlarged)

An insect's wings are often **transparent;** they are so thin you can almost see through them. Often they are **veined** and may look just like leaves. Sometimes the second pair of wings is hard, and makes a shield over the thinner wings.

The insect's body is covered with a coat made of **chitin.** Chitin is very strong and tough. It is also waterproof. As the insect grows, it sheds its coat and grows a bigger one. We say it **molts.**

In the female insect there is often an **ovipositor,** or "egg depositor." The mother insect lays eggs through her ovipositor. She may bore a hole with it to make a nest for her eggs.

WING OF CICADA
(Enlarged)

LADYBIRD WINGS
(Enlarged)

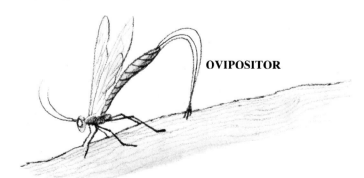

OVIPOSITOR

ICHNEUMON laying eggs

INSECTS

All insects start out as **eggs.** Some insects come out of their eggs looking just like their parents, only smaller. Others go through another stage before they turn into grown-up insects. The young of some insects at this stage are called **nymphs.**

Many insects go through a complete change from egg to **imago** (adult). This change is called **metamorphosis,** a long word which means "change of form." **Larva, grub, maggot, caterpillar,** and **wriggler** are all names for young insects going through their first stage of metamorphosis.

The **pupa** is the resting stage. Usually the larva makes a shell or jacket called a **cocoon,** or **chrysalis.** We say it **pupates.**

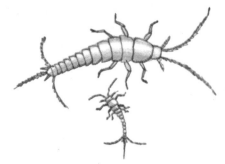

SILVERFISH AND YOUNG

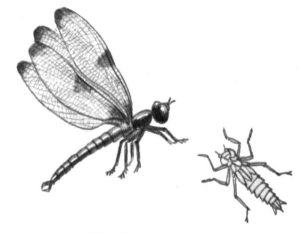

DRAGONFLY AND NYMPH

The life of a butterfly

It is exciting to see a grown-up insect finally come out of its pupal stage. It looks completely different from the way it started out. Who could guess that a caterpillar would one day turn into a beautiful butterfly?

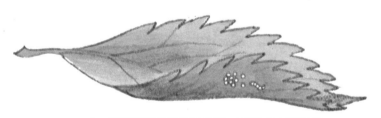

1. BUTTERFLY EGGS AND LARVAE

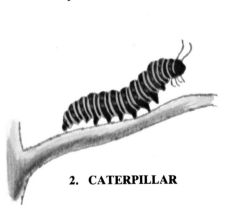

2. CATERPILLAR

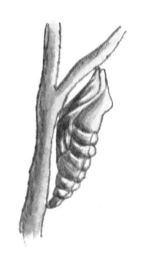

3. CHRYSALIS CONTAINING PUPA

4. ADULT BUTTERFLY EMERGING

Social insects: Bees

Many insects live alone. But some live together in **colonies.** They are called **social insects.** Ants, bees, wasps, and termites are social insects.

Honeybees live in **hives.** Each hive has a **queen bee.** She lays hundreds of eggs in **cells** made from **wax.** **Worker bees** make the cells and also gather **pollen** and **nectar** from flowers. With the pollen and nectar they make **honey** to feed the bee **larvae.**

When bees carry pollen from one flower to another we say they **pollinate** the flower. They help the flowers to make seeds so new flowers will grow.

Drones do no work in the hive. But when the queen bee leaves the hive, drones and workers **swarm** around her. They help her build a new hive.

WORKER BEE GATHERING POLLEN AND NECTAR

INSIDE A BEEHIVE

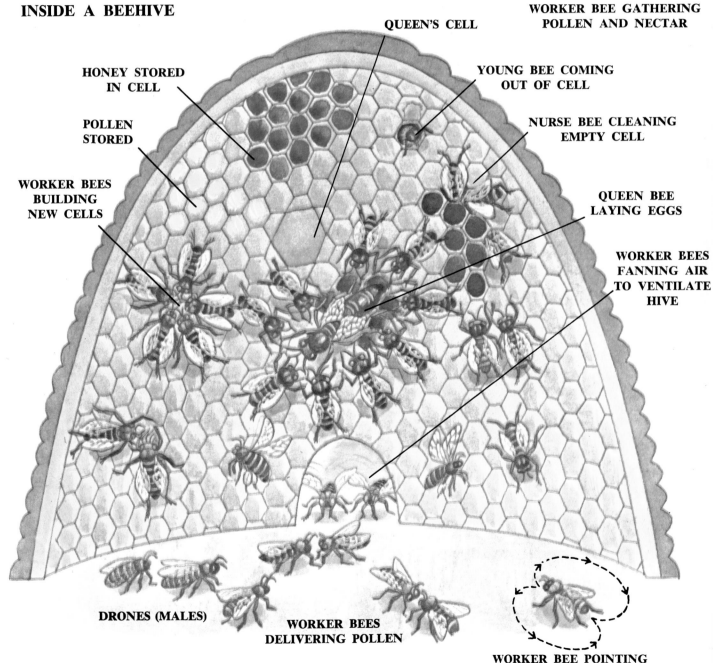

QUEEN'S CELL

HONEY STORED IN CELL

POLLEN STORED

WORKER BEES BUILDING NEW CELLS

YOUNG BEE COMING OUT OF CELL

NURSE BEE CLEANING EMPTY CELL

QUEEN BEE LAYING EGGS

WORKER BEES FANNING AIR TO VENTILATE HIVE

DRONES (MALES)

WORKER BEES DELIVERING POLLEN

WORKER BEE POINTING WAY TO FLOWER

25

INSECTS

Ants

Ants, too, are social insects. They make big **anthills,** or **mounds.** The **queen ant** lays hundreds of eggs. The **worker** and **soldier ants** look after the **grubs** until they grow up into adults.

INSIDE AN ANTHILL

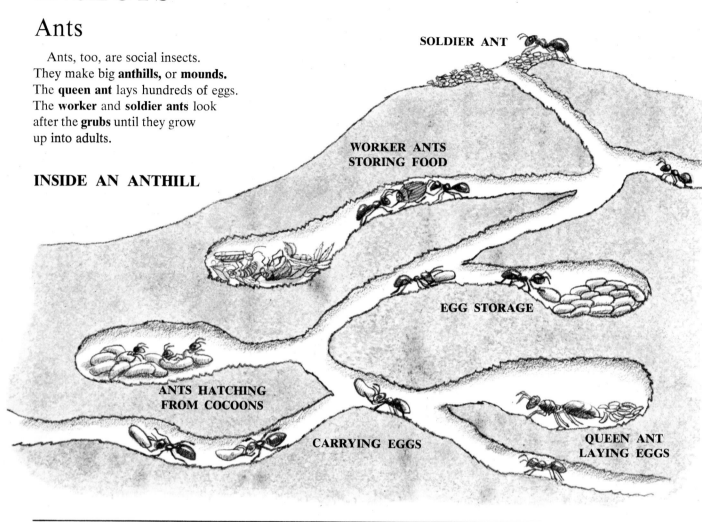

SOLDIER ANT

WORKER ANTS STORING FOOD

EGG STORAGE

ANTS HATCHING FROM COCOONS

CARRYING EGGS

QUEEN ANT LAYING EGGS

Insect pests

We call some insects **pests.** They are a nuisance to us. They sting and bite. They can be **parasites,** living on or inside other animals. They can make us very sick and can spread disease. They can eat up our food and even our houses.

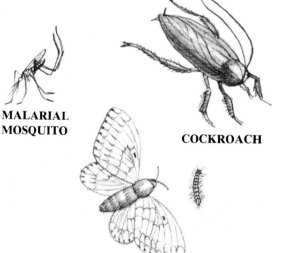

MALARIAL MOSQUITO

COCKROACH

BOLL WEEVIL

BLUEBOTTLE

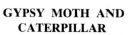

GYPSY MOTH AND CATERPILLAR

TERMITE

JAPANESE BEETLE

More insects

Many insects do no harm. Most of them are very beautiful and very interesting. They help make our world a pleasant place. They **pollinate** flowers. They make **honey.** They make **silk.** They are **food** for birds, fish, and other animals. They make pleasant **chirps.** They **glow** on a summer evening. There are hundreds and thousands of insects on this earth, many more than there are people, many more than any other animal.

WATER BEETLE

KATYDID

BUTTERFLY

BUMBLEBEE

CRICKET

APHIDS

JUNE BUG

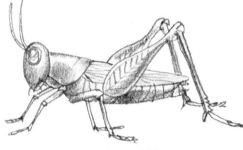

GRASSHOPPER

WASP

MAYFLY

FLEA
(Enlarged)

EARWIG

STAG BEETLE

FIREFLY

DEATH'S-HEAD MOTH

Animals (Vertebrates)
FISH

Vertebrates are animals with **backbones.** Fish are vertebrates. They live in the water. They breathe through **gills.** They swim and dive and dart around. Some fish seem to fly out of the water. Their **fins,** especially their tail fins, help them to swim. Their shape is usually **streamlined.** Their bodies are covered with **scales.**

PARTS OF A FISH

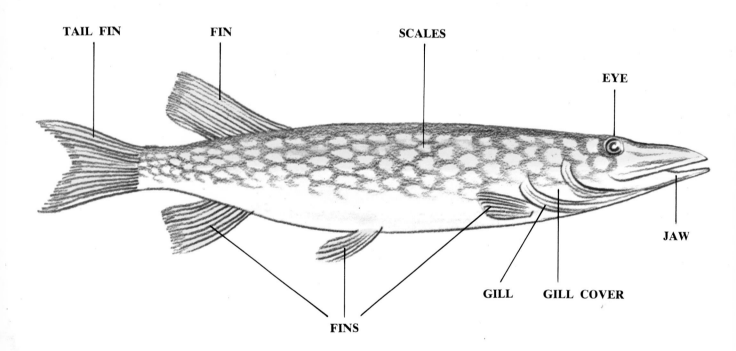

TAIL FIN   FIN   SCALES   EYE

JAW

FINS   GILL   GILL COVER

PILOTFISH follows sharks and feeds on **scraps**.

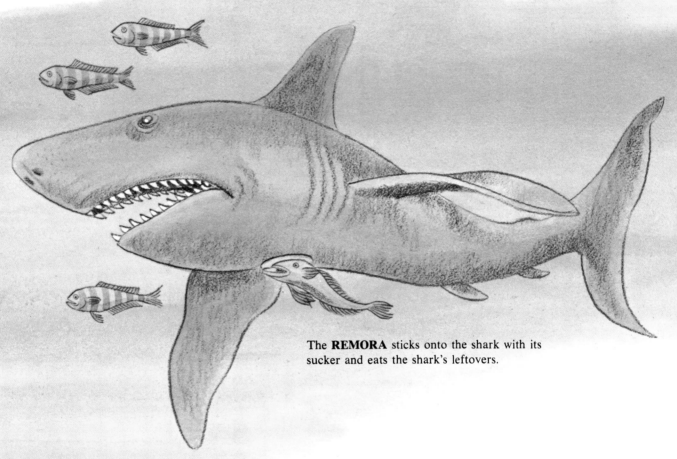

The **REMORA** sticks onto the shark with its sucker and eats the shark's leftovers.

SHARK

Fish may be very big or very small. The **goby** is only about this size: 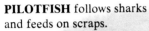 The biggest fish of all is the **shark.** Instead of bones, sharks (and some other fish) have skeletons of tough **gristle.** Instead of scales, the shark has a rough skin covered with tiny, hard knobs. A shark's skin feels like sandpaper. The shark has lots of very sharp teeth in its big jaws.

FISH
Shallow water

Some fish live among the **coral reefs,** where the water is warm and clear. Often they are brightly colored.

Deep sea

Other fish live deep down at the bottom of the sea. Sometimes they have lights along the sides of their bodies. Or they may have eyes like lanterns.

The angler catches other fish with a line and "bait."

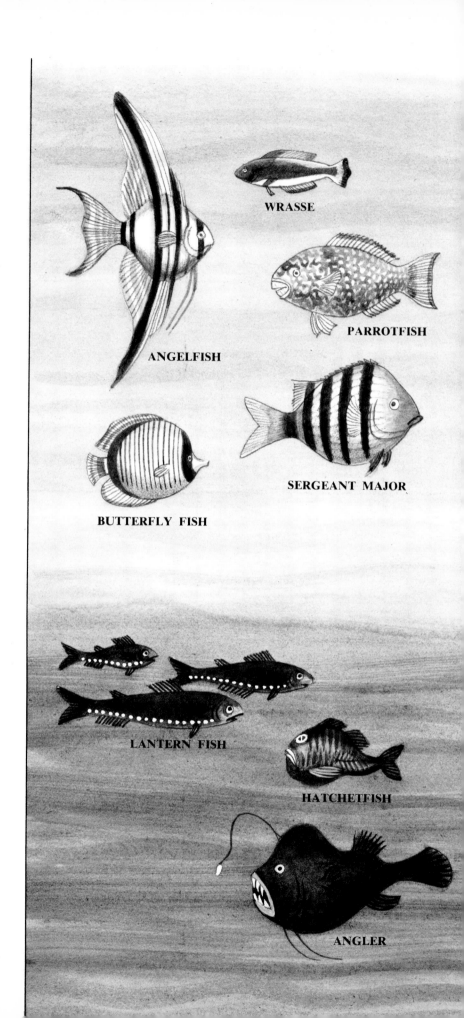

WRASSE

PARROTFISH

ANGELFISH

SERGEANT MAJOR

BUTTERFLY FISH

LANTERN FISH

HATCHETFISH

ANGLER

Salmon's journey

Some fish live only in salt water. Others live only in fresh water. Some fish spend part of their lives in fresh water and part in salt water.

The **salmon** spends most of its life in salt water. When it is ready to **spawn,** or lay eggs, it travels for many miles to the freshwater stream where it was born. A baby salmon is called a **fingerling.**

SALMON

Eel's journey

The **eel** spends most of its life in fresh water. When it is ready to **spawn,** it travels many miles to the part of the ocean where it was born. A baby eel is called an **elver.**

EEL

FISH

The eggs that a mother fish carries are called **roe.** Most fish eggs float in the water or lie on the sea bottom in jellylike blobs. But some fish take care of their young. Young fish are called **fry.**

The father **CATFISH** carries the eggs in his mouth until they hatch.

The **SEAHORSE** mother puts her eggs into the father's pouch. He looks after them until they hatch.

A PANORAMA OF FISH

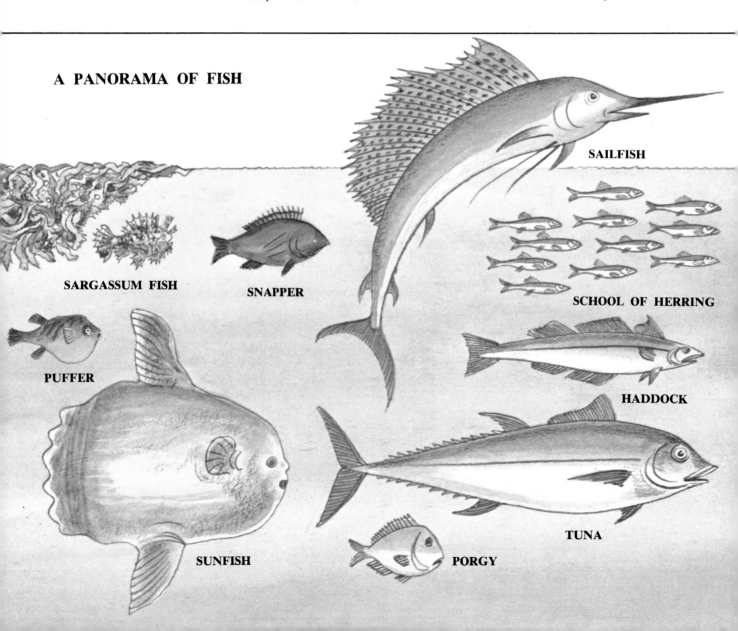

SARGASSUM FISH

SNAPPER

SAILFISH

SCHOOL OF HERRING

PUFFER

HADDOCK

SUNFISH

PORGY

TUNA

What do fish eat?

The sea may look empty, but if you look at a cupful of sea water under a microscope, look what you find: hundreds of tiny creatures and plants! They make a kind of sea soup called **plankton.** It is very good food for fishes and other sea creatures. Fish have many different eating habits. But mostly, big fish eat little fish and little fish eat smaller fish. It is fortunate there are so many fish in the sea!

STICKLEBACKS build nests for their eggs.

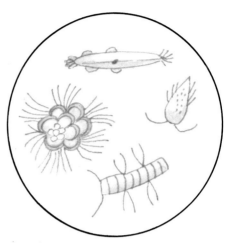

PLANKTON UNDER A MICROSCOPE

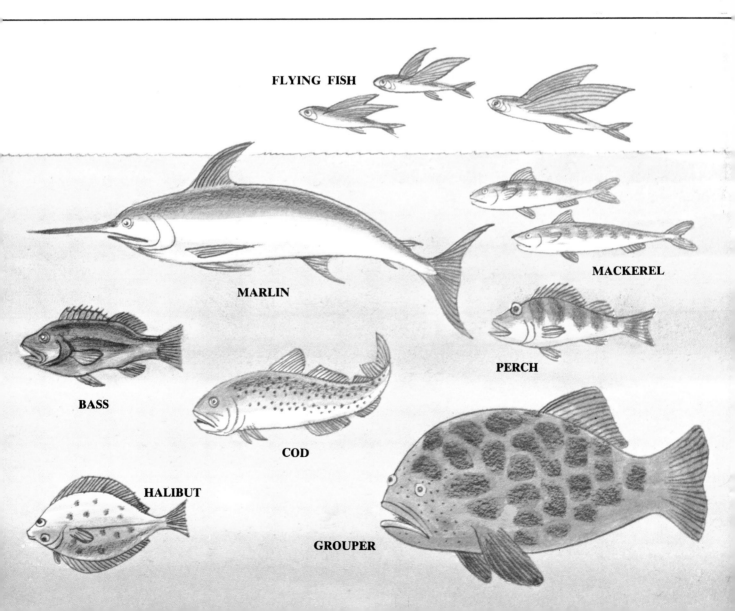

FLYING FISH

MACKEREL

MARLIN

PERCH

BASS

COD

HALIBUT

GROUPER

REPTILES

Snakes, lizards, turtles, and crocodiles are **reptiles.**
Dinosaurs of long ago were reptiles. Reptiles are
animals that are **cold blooded.** That doesn't mean that
their blood is cold all the time. It means that their
blood gets warm in the sun and cool in the shade.
Their temperature changes with the surroundings.
People and other animals are warm blooded. Their
body temperature stays more or less the same
in sunshine or rain, day or night, winter or
summer, unless they are sick.

TYRANNOSAURUS REX

All reptiles like to **bask** in the sun. You may find a turtle sunning himself on a rock by the pond. He will plop back into the water when he sees you. Reptiles spend most of their days shuttling back and forth between sunshine and shade. In winter they **hibernate.** They sleep in holes, or in logs, or under stones, until the weather gets warm again.

Most reptiles **hatch** from eggs. Reptile babies can take care of themselves right away. They do not live with their mothers or with each other.

GARTER SNAKE

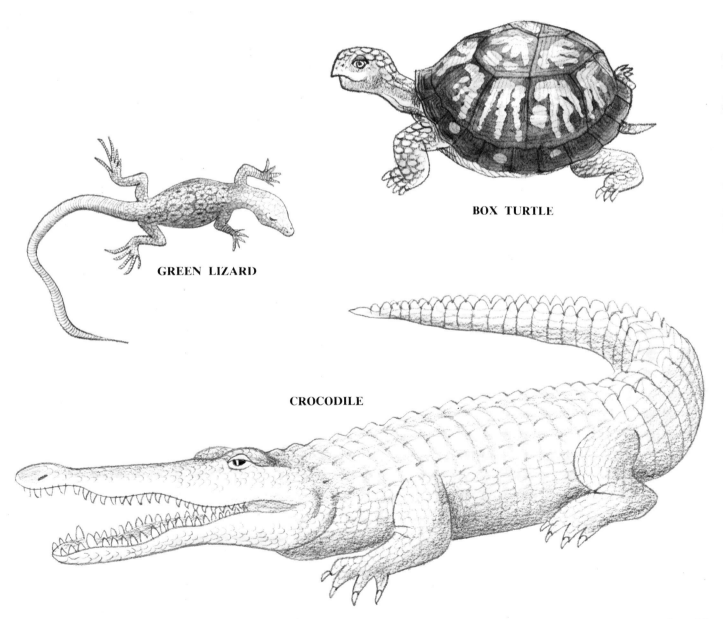

BOX TURTLE

GREEN LIZARD

CROCODILE

REPTILES
Snakes

Snakes have no legs. But they can move; snakes slink and slither. They creep and glide. Most snakes can swim and climb trees. They lie in **coils.** They **hiss** when they are scared or annoyed. A rattlesnake rattles its tail. Some snakes blow up **hoods** around their necks.

Their skins are dry and scaly. As a snake grows bigger, it grows out of its skin. It **sheds** or, **sloughs,** it and there is a handsome new skin underneath.

Some snakes can give **poisonous** bites. They have venom in their **fangs.** A snake's tongue is forked. Snakes have **flexible** jaws. They swallow their food whole without chewing. **Back-slanting** teeth help get the food down. After a snake has a large meal it usually goes to sleep for a few days. Snakes have no eyelids so they cannot blink. They sleep with their eyes open.

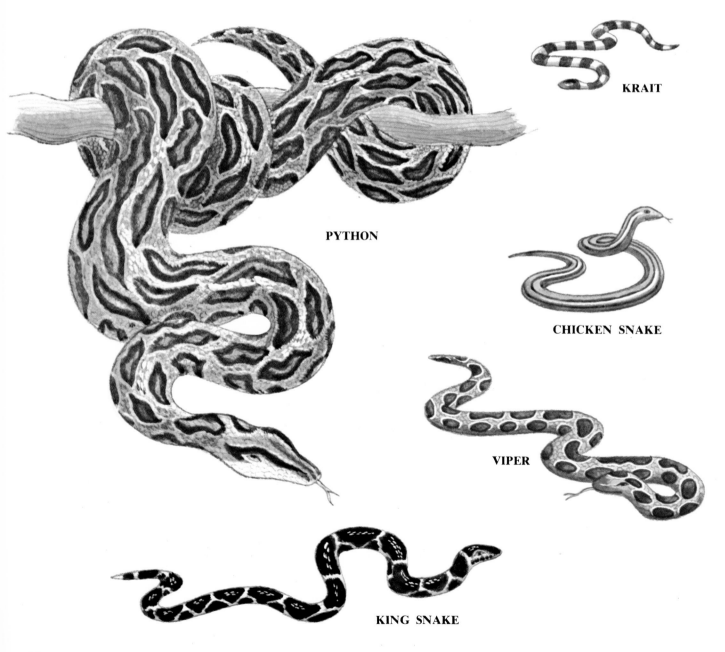

KRAIT

PYTHON

CHICKEN SNAKE

VIPER

KING SNAKE

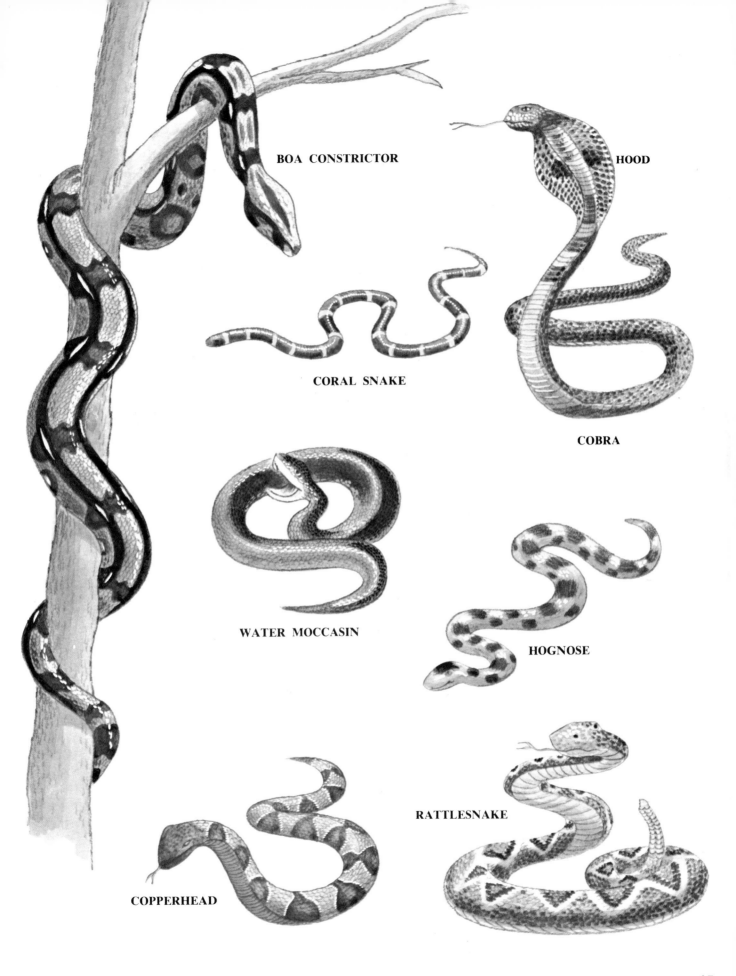

BOA CONSTRICTOR

HOOD

CORAL SNAKE

COBRA

WATER MOCCASIN

HOGNOSE

RATTLESNAKE

COPPERHEAD

REPTILES
Lizards

Lizards have legs. They move about very fast. Sometimes they run upright on their back legs, like small dinosaurs. Some have **pads** on their feet to help them climb or walk upside down. Most have **claws** on the ends of their toes. They dart out their long tongues to catch insects. They can become very friendly and good to have around.

Lizards have many ways of showing off. They may have **frilly collars, crested backs, inflatable sacs, beaded scales,** or **helmeted heads.** Some can even change their color. They puff and pant and do push-ups. Most lizards can snap off their tails and grow new ones!

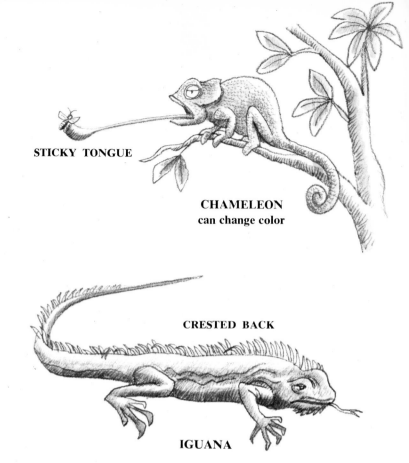

STICKY TONGUE

**CHAMELEON
can change color**

CRESTED BACK

IGUANA

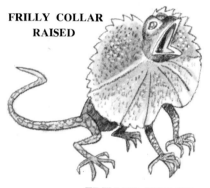

**FRILLY COLLAR
RAISED**

FRILLED LIZARD

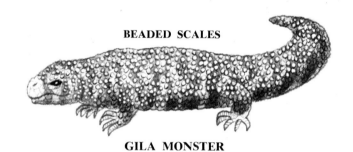

BEADED SCALES

GILA MONSTER

HORNED LIZARD

KOMODO DRAGON

GECKO

Turtles

Turtles (or **tortoises**) are the only reptiles with **shells.** Turtles cannot move very fast. But their heavy shells keep them safe from most enemies. When a turtle is inside its shell, even a bear, or a puma, or a sharp knife can't pry it open.

Turtles that spend a lot of time in the water have **webbed feet** like **flippers** that help them swim. Some freshwater turtles are called **terrapins.**

All turtles lay eggs. **Marine turtles** must come ashore to lay their eggs. It is hard for them to walk on land. But they crawl ashore, often at the time of the full moon, and dig holes with their flippers. Then they lay their eggs and cover them up and go back to the sea. Safe above the **high-tide line,** the eggs hatch. When the baby turtles come out of their shells they head straight for the water.

Turtles have no teeth. They have **horny beaks,** or **bills,** and strong jaws. A bite from a snapping turtle can hurt. But most turtles are peaceful animals that do no harm. They may live for a very long time, sometimes over a hundred years.

CARAPACE (upper shell)

PLASTRON (lower shell)

GALAPAGOS TORTOISE

SNAPPING TURTLE

MINIATURE TURTLE

HAWKSBILL TURTLE

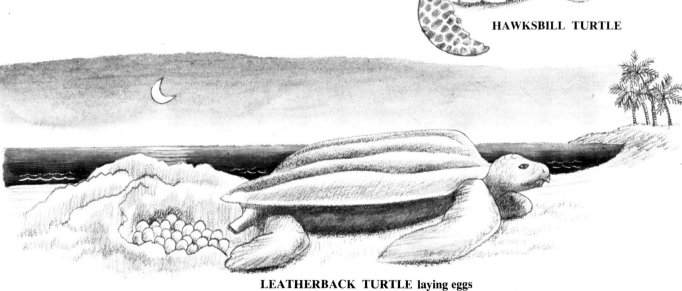

LEATHERBACK TURTLE laying eggs

REPTILES
Crocodilians

Crocodilians is a word we use when we mean everyone in the **crocodile** family: **alligators, gavials** from India and Malaysia, **caimans** and **jacares** from South America, and, of course, **crocodiles.**

They look like big lizards. They have long, strong tails, short stubby legs, and webbed feet. They always live near water and spend a lot of time floating near the surface, **basking** in the sun and looking like logs, until suddenly the big jaws open and show the sharp teeth.

Crocodilians eat all kinds of birds, and bird's eggs, fish, and other animals.

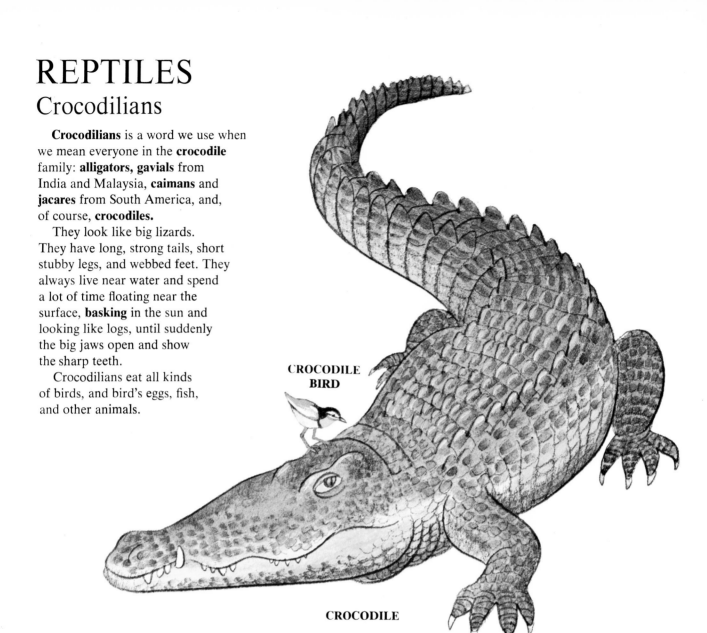

CROCODILE BIRD

CROCODILE

GAVIAL

Alligators

The alligator mother is one of the few reptiles that stays around to see her babies hatch. She makes a big mound of leaves and mud. She keeps the mud wet. When she hears the babies grunt, she goes to help them out of the nest. But she does not stay with them long.

ALLIGATOR WITH HATCHING EGGS

How to tell the difference between a crocodile and an alligator

A crocodile is longer and slimmer than an alligator. The crocodile has a bigger bulge over each yellow-green eye. Two of the crocodile's teeth show even when its mouth is closed. The alligator's teeth all fit inside its mouth.

Alligators are found only in Florida and in China. Crocodiles are found in many more places, including Africa, Asia, and South America.

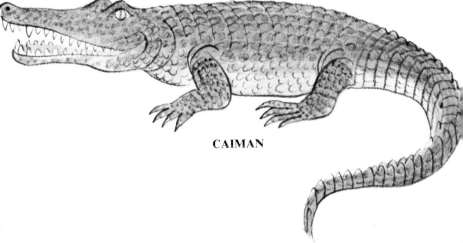

CAIMAN

AMPHIBIANS

The word **amphibian** means "two lives." Amphibians start life in the water, like fish. When they grow up, they live on land. But they still spend a lot of time in or near water. They are at home in both places. **Frogs, toads,** and **salamanders** are amphibians.

BULLFROG

Life cycle of the frog

Frogs and toads lay their jellylike eggs in the water. Out of the eggs come tiny **larvae.** These little creatures cling onto underwater weeds and start to grow. Soon the larvae change to **tadpoles,** or **polliwogs.** They have big heads and long tails. They live under water, swimming about and breathing through **gills** like fish.

As they grow bigger, they begin to grow legs. Their tails get shorter as their legs get longer. They begin to grow **lungs.** Now they must come above the water to breathe. When the tail has completely disappeared and the legs are long and strong, frogs and toads are grown-up. They leave the water and live on land.

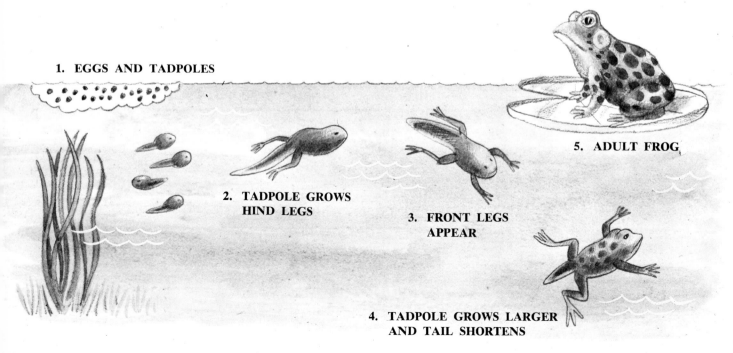

1. EGGS AND TADPOLES

2. TADPOLE GROWS HIND LEGS

3. FRONT LEGS APPEAR

4. TADPOLE GROWS LARGER AND TAIL SHORTENS

5. ADULT FROG

Frogs and toads

Wherever there is a pond or a lake, frogs and toads are sure to be there. They make a lot of noise. They **croak, bark, boom, chirp, peep,** and **trill.** The bullfrog has a deep voice that seems to say "jug-a-rum." He has **inflatable air sacs** like balloons that help make the sound.

Both toads and frogs have long, strong legs and **webbed** toes. They have no claws. They have long, sticky tongues. They catch insects by darting their tongues out. It is good to have a frog or a toad in your garden to catch insects.

Both toads and frogs **hibernate.** When the cold weather comes, they burrow under the mud. Or they find deep holes under leaves or moss or rocks. They sleep until spring.

INFLATABLE SAC

TOAD

TREE FROGS

How to tell the difference between frogs and toads

A frog's skin is moist and smooth. A toad's skin is drier and may be warty. A toad moves slowly. It only hops sometimes. A frog makes long, light leaps. Toads come out mostly at night. They wander farther from the water than frogs.

AMPHIBIANS
Newts and salamanders

Newts and **salamanders** look a lot like lizards. But they are **amphibians,** not reptiles. They do not have scales. Their skin is moist and soft. They must keep it damp and cool all the time. They have no claws on their toes. They cannot snap off their tails as lizards can. They do not have long tongues. They catch insects in their mouths.

Salamanders start life in the water as eggs covered with **jelly.** Out of the eggs come **larvae,** which change into **tadpoles.** They breathe under water through feathery-looking **gills.** Their tails get very long. They grow short legs. Finally, they grow **lungs** and must come above water to breathe. Then, at last, they come ashore to live. In winter they **hibernate.**

A newt is a kind of salamander. A young newt that has just come ashore is an **eft.**

LIFE CYCLE OF THE NEWT

ADULT

EFT

EGGS

TADPOLES

GILLS

BIRDS

Birds have **wings.** Birds **fly.**
They flap their wings. They soar.
They swoop. They glide. Some birds
dive. Little birds flutter.
Hummingbirds hover like tiny
helicopters. Ostriches and penguins
and a few other birds cannot fly
at all.

Birds' bodies are covered with
feathers. A bird's feathers are
sometimes called **plumage.** A bird
keeps its feathers clean by **preening,**
bathing, and by taking **dust baths.**
When birds **molt,** they lose their
old feathers and grow new ones.

GOLDEN EAGLE
soaring

HAWK gliding

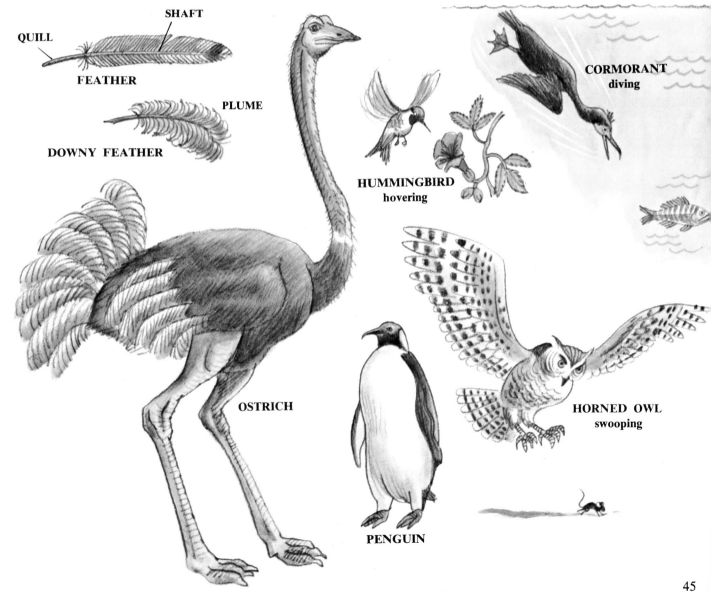

QUILL

SHAFT

FEATHER

PLUME

DOWNY FEATHER

HUMMINGBIRD
hovering

CORMORANT
diving

OSTRICH

PENGUIN

HORNED OWL
swooping

45

BIRDS

Some birds have **tufts,** or **crests,** or **crowns** on their heads. Birds have large, sharp eyes that can see clearly, even from high up. They have a third **eyelid** like a clear glass windshield, to protect their eyes when they are flying.

TUFTED TITMOUSE

BLUEJAY

TOUCAN

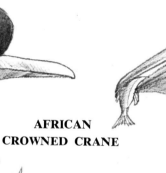

CREST

AFRICAN CROWNED CRANE

POUCH

Birds have **beaks,** or **bills:** long beaks, good for digging; sturdy beaks, good for cracking seeds; beaks with **pouches,** fine for storing fish; strong, pointed beaks, for making holes.

PELICAN

FLICKER making hole in tree

HAWK with prey

ROBIN pulling up worm

Some birds **peck** at seeds and fruit and worms. Others are **birds of prey,** or **predators.** They hunt small animals, birds, and fish. Some sip **nectar.** Some eat **carrion,** or dead animals. They are **scavengers.**

VULTURE with carrion

Birds have two legs. Sometimes their feet are **webbed** to help them swim. Other birds have strong **talons** so they can hold their food. Others, like the swift, have tiny feet. They hardly ever perch. Some birds have long legs. They can **wade** in shallow water. Birds' toes are sometimes called **claws.**

WEB FOOT

GOOSE

PARROT

TALONS

CHIMNEY SWIFT

CARDINAL perching

BLUE HERON
wading

CHICKEN roosting

When birds take a quick rest, we say they **perch.** When they settle down for a longer time, we say they **roost.**

BIRDS

Birds build different kinds of **nests.** Big nests, middle-sized nests, tiny nests, or just hollows in the ground. They **lay eggs** in their nests. The mother or father bird sits on the eggs to keep them warm, or protect them from the sun. They **incubate** the eggs. The father bird is a **cock.** The mother bird is a **hen.** When the eggs hatch, baby birds come out of them. They are **nestlings,** or **chicks.** When the bird babies learn to fly they are called **fledglings.**

HUMMINGBIRD NEST

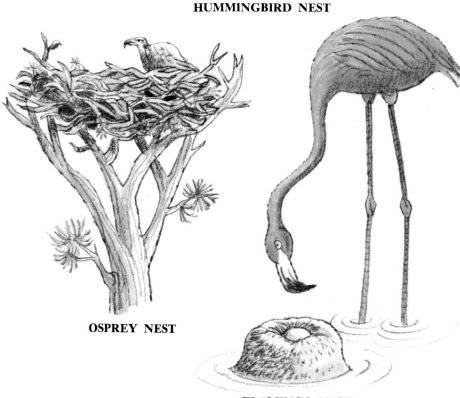

OSPREY NEST

FLAMINGO NEST

BARN SWALLOW NEST

SWANS

PEN

COB

CYGNETS

DUCK

DUCKLINGS

Swans have special names. The mother is a **pen.** The father is a **cob.** Baby swans are called **cygnets.** Little ducks are **ducklings.** Little geese are **goslings.**

Birds **sing.** They **warble** and **twitter,** **cheep** and **trill.** They cry "caw! caw!" or "cuckoo!" or "whoo-ooo?" They **mew** and **cackle** and **screech.**

SPARROW
"cheep"

KOOKABURRA
"cackle"

MEADOWLARK
"trill"

CROW
"caw"

CUCKOO
"cuckoo"

OWL
"who-oo"

COCKATOO
"screech"

CATBIRD
"mew"

CANARY
"warble"

CANADA GEESE MIGRATING

Many birds fly away when autumn winds blow, and there's not enough food, and it's cold. We say they **migrate.** They come back again in spring and we are happy to see them once more.

49

MAMMALS

The animals that we know best are **mammals.** Mammals have **backbones,** or **vertebrae.** The backbone is called a **spine.** Mammals have four **limbs** (arms and legs), except for the **aquatic** (water) mammals.

Mammals' bodies are covered with fine **hair** or thick **fur.** They are **warm blooded,** which means that their temperature remains more or less the same, no matter what the weather.

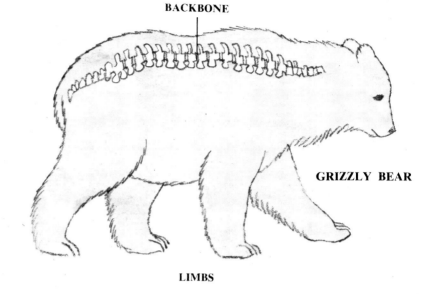

BACKBONE

GRIZZLY BEAR

LIMBS

ECHIDNA

DUCKBILL PLATYPUS

Mammal babies are born live, not as eggs. Only the duckbill platypus, the echidna, and a few rare relatives lay eggs.

Mammals **nurse** their babies. The mothers feed them with milk from their bodies. They take care of them until they are grown.

The cow's **UDDER** contains milk for her baby calf.

Parts of a mammal

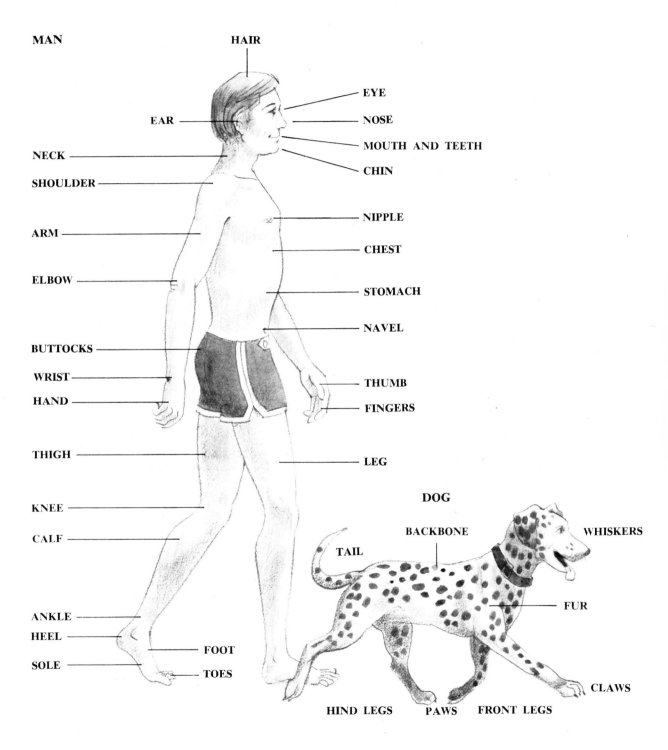

MAN

HAIR

EYE

NOSE

EAR

MOUTH AND TEETH

CHIN

NECK

SHOULDER

NIPPLE

ARM

CHEST

ELBOW

STOMACH

NAVEL

BUTTOCKS

WRIST

THUMB

HAND

FINGERS

THIGH

LEG

DOG

KNEE

BACKBONE

WHISKERS

CALF

TAIL

FUR

ANKLE

HEEL

FOOT

SOLE

TOES

CLAWS

HIND LEGS

PAWS

FRONT LEGS

Other mammals have **trunks** and **tusks**, **antlers** and **horns**, **pouches** and **manes**, **hoofs** and **flippers**. You'll see them under **Families of Mammals.**

51

What mammals wear

ZEBRA

Stripes

LEOPARD

Spots

BEAR

Shaggy coat

GAZELLE

Sleek coat

ELEPHANT

Tough coat

ARMADILLO

Armored coat

SHEEP

Woolly coat

PORCUPINE

Bristly coat

KOALA

Soft, furry coat

YAK

Long-haired coat

OTTER

Short-haired coat

SEAL

Waterproof coat

PIG

Curly tail

PONY

Pony tail

LION

Tufted tail

MONKEY

Long tail

PANDA

Short tail

BOBCAT

Bob tail

RABBIT

Cotton tail

SQUIRREL

Bushy tail

A dog wags his tail to show he is pleased.

A beaver sounds a warning with his flat tail.

A fox warms his nose with his bushy tail.

To signal danger, a deer flicks up its white tail.

Some moving words

BATS FLY	**PEOPLE WALK**	**HORSES GALLOP**	**DOLPHINS DIVE**
APES SWING	**RABBITS HOP**	**WEASELS SLINK**	**RATS SCURRY**
SLOTHS HANG	**KANGAROOS LEAP**	**MOLES DIG**	Animal **footprints** are also called **tracks, pugmarks,** and **spoor.**

Noisy words

DOGS BARK	**LIONS ROAR**	**CATS MEW**	**COWS MOO**
HORSES NEIGH	**SHEEP BAA**	**PIGS OINK**	**WOLVES HOWL**
ELEPHANTS TRUMPET	**MONKEYS CHATTER**	**MICE SQUEAK**	**HYENAS LAUGH**

FAMILIES OF MAMMALS
Primates

Primates include **human beings** and our closest relatives, the **apes.** Smaller than the apes are many kinds of monkeys, such as the rhesus, the capuchin, the baboon, and the long-tailed spider monkey.

Nearly all the primates are tree-dwellers. They have big brains and are very smart. **Thumbs** help them to grasp branches of trees, to peel fruit, and sometimes to use tools.

CAPUCHIN MONKEY

GIBBON

GORILLA

CHIMPANZEE

MAN

RHESUS MONKEY

SPIDER MONKEY

ORANGUTAN

BABOON

Dogs

The dogs and cats that we keep as **pets** have many wild cousins.

A young dog is a PUPPY.

COYOTE

WOLF

JACKAL

FOX

DINGO

Cats

MANE

LIONESS

LION

CUB

A PRIDE OF LIONS

TIGER

MOUNTAIN LION — also called **PUMA, COUGAR,** and **CATAMOUNT**

LEOPARD

JAGUAR

HOUSE CAT

CHEETAH

LYNX

A pleased cat purrs.

KITTENS

FAMILIES OF MAMMALS

Rodents

There are hundreds of kinds of **rodents,** or **gnawers.** They all have teeth especially good for chomping on seeds, tree barks, and plants.

RAT

MOUSE

HARE

PORCUPINE

SQUIRREL

CHIPMUNK

BEAVER

Ungulates

These are hoofed animals, or **ungulates.**

MANE

STAG **FAWN** **DOE**

DEER

HORSE

COW

ZEBRA

GIRAFFE

RHINOCEROS

YAK

Aquatic mammals

Some mammals are **aquatic.** They live in the water, but they must come up to breathe, and they nurse their young like all mammals.

SEAL

TUSKS

WALRUS

SPOUT

FLUKED TAIL

WHALE
The blue whale is the biggest of all animals.

PORPOISE

DOLPHIN

Marsupials

Marsupials are mammals with **pouches.** Their babies are born very tiny. They must live in the mother's pouch until they grow bigger. Marsupials live mostly in Australia. But the opossum lives in North America; you may see a mother opossum carrying her babies on her back.

OPOSSUM

KANGAROO

KOALA

GLOSSARY-INDEX

In addition to helping you look up plants and animals in the book, this special Glossary-Index will help to explain some of the words used. Where pronunciation is unusual, the word is spelled, in brackets, the way it sounds.

A

Abalone, 18

Abdomen: The part of an animal that usually contains the digestive organs.

Alga (plural algae, pronounced **al**-jee), 13, 14

Alligator, 41

Ameba or Amoeba: Tiny, one-celled animal, 17

Amphibian (am-**fi**-bi-an): A cold-blooded animal that spends its early life under water, develops lungs and lives mostly on land, 42-44

Angel fish, 30

Angler, 30

Animals, 16-57; amphibians, 42-44; arachnids, 20; birds, 45-49; crustaceans, 19; fish, 28-33; insects, 21-27; invertebrates, 16-27; mammals, 50-57; reptiles, 34-41; vertebrates, 28-57. See individual names.

Ankle: The joint between the foot and the leg.

Ant, 23, 25, 26

Antenna (an-**ten**-a; plural antennae): Sensitive feelers on the heads of insects, crustaceans, and snails.

Anther: The pollen-bearing part of the stamen, or male part, of a flower, 10

Antler: Bony growth on the head of a deer, shed once a year, 56

Ape, 53, 54

Aphid, 27

Apple, 8, 11

Aquatic: Living in water. Aquatic animals include fish, crustaceans, and certain insects and mammals.

Arachnids: Animals, such as spiders and scorpions, that look like insects but have eight legs instead of six, 20

Arm: 1) One of the upper or fore limbs of an animal; 2) One of the limbs of a tree.

Armadillo, 52

Asp, 37

Autumn or Fall: The season of the year between summer and winter.

B

Baboon, 54

Backbone: The column of bones (the spine) that forms the main support of the animals called vertebrates.

Bark: 1) The tough, outer covering of a tree trunk, 12, 56; 2) The sound made by animals such as dogs, 53

Bask: To enjoy the warmth of the sun.

Bass, 33

Bat, 53

Beak: The hard mouth part, often pointed, of a bird, insect, or other animal.

Bear, 50, 52

Beaver, 52, 56

Bee, 10, 23, 25, 27

Beetles: Group of insects that have a tough leathery pair of wings that folds over the back pair of wings when not flying.

Belly button: See Navel

Bill: See Beak

Birds, 45-49. See individual names.

Bivalve: A mollusk that has two shells hinged together, 18

Black widow, 20

Blood: see Cold blooded, Warm blooded.

Bluebottle, 26

Bluejay, 46

Boa constrictor, 37

Bobcat, 52

Boll weevil, 26

Box turtle, 35

Branch: An arm growing from the trunk of a tree, 12

Bud: An unopened leaf or flower, 13

Bugs; Group of insects with mouths especially well made for piercing and sucking.

Bullfrog, 42

Butterfly, 21, 24, 27

Butterfly fish, 30

Buttocks: The round, fleshy part of the lower back.

Button: First part of the mushroom to appear above the ground, 14

C

Cactus, 9

Caiman, 40, 41

Calf (kaf, plural, calves): 1) The young of certain animals, e.g. cows, whales; 2) The part of the leg between knee and ankle.

Calyx: The part of the flower made up by the sepals, 10

Canary, 49

Capuchin monkey, 54

Carapace: Hard outer covering, or shell, of animals such as turtles and lobsters, 19, 39

Cardinal, 47

Carrion: Dead, decaying animal, 46

Carrot, 9

Cat, 53, 55

Catamount, 55

Catbird, 49

Catfish, 32

Cattail, 9

Caterpillar: The larva, or young, of a butterfly or moth, 24

Celery, 8

Cell: 1) Smallest unit of plant or animal life; 2) Part of a honeycomb.

Cephalopods (se-**fa**-lo-pods): A group of sea animals that have heads and tentacles, 18

Chameleon (ka-**me**-le-on), 38

Cheetah, 55

Cherry, 11

Chest: The part of the body enclosed by the ribs.

Chick: A baby bird.

Chicken, 47

Chimpanzee, 54

Chin: The middle part of the lower jaw.

Chipmunk, 56

Chitin (**ky**-tin): Hard, waterproof material that makes up outer covering of insects and crustaceans.

Chrysalis (**cris**-sa-lis): The pupal, or resting, stage of a young butterfly or moth, 24

Cicada, 23

Clam, 18

Claw: 1) Sharp, curved nail of an animal such as the cat; 2) Large, grasping "arm" of crab or lobster.

Cob: Male, adult swan, 48

Cobra, 37

Cock: a male bird.

Cockatoo, 49

Cockroach, 26

Coconut, 9

Cocoon: The covering around the pupa of an insect such as the moth, 20, 24

Cod, 33

Cold blooded, 34, 50

Compound eye: An eye, such as some insects', made up of hundreds of light-reflecting lenses. A simple eye, such as a person's, has only one lens.

Cone shell, 17

Conch, 18

Copperhead, 37

Corals: Small, underwater animals whose hard skeletons form coral reefs, 16, 17, 30

Coral snake, 37

Cormorant, 45

Corn, 9

Cotyledon (cotty-**leed**-on): A leaf inside the seed that contains food for the new plant. It is usually the first leaf to show above ground. It is sometimes called a seed leaf, 11, 13

Cougar, 55

Cowrie, 17

Coyote, 55

Crab, 19

Crane, 46

Cricket, 23, 27

Crocodile, 34, 40-41

Crow, 49

Crustacean (crus-**tay**-she-on): A sea animal, such as the lobster, whose body is covered with a shell, 19

Cub: A young animal, especially of the cat or bear family.

Cuckoo, 49

Cuttlefish, 18

Cygnet: Baby swan, 48

D

Daddy longlegs (or Harvestman), 20

Daisy, 8

Dandelion, 11

Death's head moth, 27

Deer, 52, 56

Digestion: The process in which the stomach and other organs change food into a form easily absorbed by the body.

Dingo, 55

Dinosaur: Large reptile that lived on earth millions of years ago, 34, 38

Diving beetle, 23

Doe: Female deer or rabbit.

Dog, 51, 52, 53, 55

Dolphin, 53, 57

Dragonfly, 21, 24

Down: The soft, under-feathers of a bird, 45

Drone: Male bee that does no work in the hive, 25

Duck, 48

Duckbill platypus, 50

E

Eagle, 45

Ear: The organ of the body that hears.

Earwig, 27

Echidna (eh-**kid**-na), 50; (Also called Spiny Anteater)

Eel, 31

Eft: Young newt, 44

Egg: Cell containing the beginning of new life, often hatched outside the mother's body, 23, 24, 25, 26, 31, 32, 35, 39, 41, 42, 44, 48, 50

Elbow: The joint between the upper and lower arm.

Elephant, 52, 53

Elver: A young eel, 31

Embryo: Earliest stage of growth after the egg cell.

Eye: The organ with which an animal sees. Look up Compound Eye.

Eyelid: The covering that comes down over the eye.

F

Fall: see Autumn.

Family: A group of related plants or animals.

Fang: A long, pointed tooth. It sometimes contains poison, 20, 37

Fawn: Baby deer, 56

Feathers: Downy covering of a bird's body, 35, 45

Female: Animal or plant that makes the egg cells from which young will grow.

Fern, 9, 12, 15

Fertilize: To join male sperm or pollen to female egg cell of animal or plant so that young will grow.

Fiddlehead: The frond of a fern before it has unfurled, 15

Filament: The stalklike part of the stamen, or male part, of a flower, 10

Fin: Part of a fish's body, including its tail, that helps it to swim, 28

Fingerling: A young fish, especially salmon or trout.

Fingers: Long, bony extensions of the hand.

Firefly, 27

Fish, 28-33. See individual names.

Flagella (fla-**jel**-la): Thin threads ("whips") that some one-celled animals lash back and forth when moving about, 17

Flamingo, 48

Flea, 27

Fledgling (**flej**-ling): Young bird that is learning to fly.

Flicker, 46

Flipper: Wide, flat part of a water animal, such as the seal, that helps it to swim.

Flowering plants, 8-13. See individual names.

Flying fish, 33

Foot: The lowest part of the leg. It rests on the ground in standing and walking.

Fox, 52, 55

Frilled lizard, 38

Frog, 42-43

Frond: The leaf of a fern or of a palm tree.

Fruit: The part of a plant that contains the fertilized seeds, 11

Fry: Newly hatched fish.

Fungus (**fung**-gus; plural, funji, pronounced **fun**-jye): Group of non-flowering plants, including mushrooms and mildew, 12, 14

Fur: The soft, warm covering on the bodies of many animals.

G

Galapagos tortoise, 39

Garter snake, 35, 36

Gavial, 40

Gazelle, 52

Gecko, 38

Gibbon, 54

Gila monster (**hee**la), 38

Gill (hard g): 1) The breathing organ of most animals that live in the water. 2) Thin blades on the underside of mushroom caps. They hold the spores, 14

Giraffe, 56

Goose (plural, geese), 47, 49

Goby, 29

Gorilla, 54

Gosling: Young goose

Gossamer: Fine, silky threads spun by spider, 20

Grape, 9

Grasshopper, 23, 27

Green lizard, 35

Gristle (**gris**-sel): Tough, elastic tissue that connects muscles and bones. It makes up the entire skeleton of fishes such as sharks, 29

Grouper, 33

Grub: The larva or young of certain insects, such as beetles, 24, 26

H

Haddock, 33

Hair: The fine, soft covering that grows from the skin of mammals. In people, it grows especially on the head.

Halibut, 33

Hand: Extension of the arm below the wrist. With fingers and thumb, it is used for seizing and holding.

Hare, 56

Harvestman, 20

Hatch: To come out of an egg.

Hatchet fish, 30

Hawk, 45, 46

Hawksbill turtle, 39

Head: The topmost, or forwardmost, part of the body. It contains the brain.

Heel: The back part of the foot.

Hen: A female bird, 48

Heron, 47

Herring, 32

Hibernate: To spend the winter asleep.

Hive: The home of a colony of bees, 25

Hognose snake, 37

Honey: The sweet mixture of nectar and pollen that bees make to feed their young, 25

Honeybee, 23, 25

Honeycomb: The waxy cells that bees make in their hives, 25

Hoof (plural, hoofs or hooves): The hard covering on the feet of animals such as horses and deer.

Horn: Hard, pointed growth on head of animals such as bulls, 56

Horned lizard, 38

Horse, 53, 56

Horseshoe crab, 19

Housefly, 21

Human body, 51

Hummingbird, 45, 48

Hyena, 53

I

Ichneumon, 23

Iguana, 38

Imago (i-**mah**-go): The fully developed, adult form of an insect.

Incubate: To keep eggs at the right temperature until they hatch, 48

"Ink": A dark liquid squirted out by the octopus and other sea animals. The inky cloud makes them hard for their enemies to see, 18-19

Insects, 21-27. See individual names.

Invertebrate: An animal with no backbone, such as an insect or a jellyfish, 16-27

J

Jacare, 40

Jackal, 55

Jaguar, 55

Japanese beetle, 26

Jaws: Bony framework of an animal's mouth.

Jellyfish, 17

Jingle shell, 18

Joint: The place where two movable parts of the body come together, e.g. knee.

June bug, 27

K

Kangaroo, 53, 57

Katydid, 27

King snake, 36

Kitten: Young cat, 55

Knee: The joint between the upper (thigh) and lower (calf) parts of the leg.

Koala, 52, 57

Komodo dragon, 38

Kookaburra, 49

Krait, 37

L

Ladybird (or Ladybug), 21, 23

Lantern fish, 30

Larva (plural, larvae): The newly hatched young of certain animals, such as insects and fish, 16, 24, 25, 42, 43, 44

Leaf (plural, leaves): Part of a plant, usually green, that helps make the plant's food, 12

Leatherback turtle, 39

Legs: Limbs used by animals in walking.

Lens: Part of the eye that focuses light rays.

Leopard, 52, 55

Salmon (**sam**-mon), 31

Sap: The liquid inside a plant that carries food, 12

Sapling: Young tree

Sargassum fish, 32

Scale: One of the thin plates that makes up the outer covering of fish and reptiles.

Scallop, 18

Scavenger: Animal that eats remains of dead animals, 46

School: Large group of fish or other sea animals traveling together, 32

Scorpion, 20

Scum: Slimy film that forms on water, often made up of algae, 14

Sea anemone, 16

Sea cucumber, 16

Seahorse, 32

Seal, 52, 57

Sea urchin, 17

Seaweed, 8, 14

Seed: Part of a flowering plant that holds the embryo, or new plant, 10, 11, 13, 25, 56

Seed leaf: Leaf inside the seed that contains food for the new plant. It is usually the first leaf to show above ground. Also called cotyledon, 11, 13

Sepal: One of the leaflike parts that makes up the outer covering of a flower, 10

Sergeant major, 30

Shark, 29

Sheep, 52

Shell: Hard outer covering of seed or animal, 11, 13, 17, 18, 19, 39

Shoal: Large group, or school, of sea animals traveling together, 32

Shoulder: The part of the body between the neck and the arm.

Shrimp, 19

Shrub: A woody, many stemmed plant, smaller than a tree.

Silverfish, 24

Skeleton: The bony, supporting framework of a vertebrate's body.

Skin: The outer covering of the body of an animal or of a fruit.

Sloth, 53

Slough (sluff): To cast off, especially a snake's skin, 35, 36

Snail, 17, 18

Snakes, 34, 36-37. See individual names.

Snapper, 32

Snapping turtle, 39

Sole: The bottom part of the foot.

Sparrow, 49

Spawn: To lay eggs in the water, 31

Spider, 19, 20

Spider monkey, 54

Spinneret: Small opening from which comes the silk for spiders to make their webs, 20

Spiny anteater: See Echidna.

Sponge, 16

Spoor: An animal's footprint, 53

Spore: Tiny, dustlike speck from which non-flowering plants reproduce, 13, 14

Spring: The season of the year between winter and summer.

Squid, 18

Squirrel, 11, 52, 56

Stag: Adult, male deer, 56

Stag beetle, 27

Stalk (stawk): Supporting part of a leaf or flower, 10, 12

Stamen: The male part of a flower that bears the pollen, 10

Starfish, 16

Stem: The main supporting part of a plant, 12, 14

Stickleback, 33

Stigma: The sticky, top part of the pistil, 10

Sting: Needlelike part of an insect that can inject poison into enemies, 22

Stink bug, 21

Stomach (**stum**-mak): The baglike organ in an animal's body where food is digested.

Strawberry, 8

Style: The tubelike part of the pistil, 10

Sucker: Mouthlike part on an·animal or plant that clings onto something else by suction, 18

Summer: The season of the year between spring and fall.

Sundial snail, 17

Sunfish, 32

Swallow, 48

Swan, 48

Swarm: Large group of insects flying together.

Swift, 47

T

Tadpole: Frog, toad, or salamander in its early life when it lives in water, 42, 44

Tail: End part of an animal's backbone, often extending beyond the body.

Talon: (**tal**-lon): Strong claw of an animal, 47

Tap root: Main root of a plant. It grows straight down from the stem, 11

Tarantula, 20

Teat: The part of a female animal's breast or udder where the baby suckles milk. See Nipple.

Temperature: The hotness or coldness of an animal's body or of its surroundings.

Tentacles: Long, flexible arms used for grasping and moving, 18

Termite, 25, 26

Terrapin: Freshwater turtle, 39

Thigh (thi): The upper part of the leg, above the knee.

Thorax: Part of the body between the head and the abdomen.

Thumb (thum): Short, thick finger of the hand that can be moved opposite each of the other fingers. Only primates have opposing thumbs.

Tiger, 55

Tiger cowrie, 17

Titmouse, 46

Toad, 42, 43

Toadstool: Mushroom, often poisonous, 14

Toe: One of the bony extensions of the foot.

Tongue (tung): Organ inside an animal's mouth, used in tasting and talking.

Tooth (plural, teeth): Bony structures in an animal's mouth, used in biting and chewing.

Tortoise, 39

Toucan, 46

Tree, 12, 13

Tree snail, 17

Tree toad, 43

Triton, 17

Trunk: 1) Woody main stem of tree, 12; 2) The main part of the body, without head or limbs; 3) A long, flexible extension of an animal's nose.

Tulip, 8

Tuna, 32

Turret, 17

Turtle, 34, 35, 39

Tusk: Long, pointed tooth.

Twig: Small shoot on branch of tree or shrub, 12

Tyrannosaurus rex, 34

U

Udder: Baglike part of female animal, such as cow. It contains milk for the animal baby to suckle, 50

Ungulate: Animal, such as horse, that has hoofed feet, 56

Univalve, 18

V

Valve: The shell of a mollusk, 18

Vein: 1) A sort of tube that carries blood in an animal's body; 2) Part of the netlike structure of a leaf or of an insect wing.

Venom: Poison, 37

Vertebrate: Animal with a backbone, 28-57

Viper, 36

Vulture, 46

W

Walkingstick, 21

Walrus, 57

Warm blooded, 34, 50

Wasp, 25, 27

Water beetle, 27

Waterlily, 11

Watermelon, 9

Water moccasin, 36

Wax: 1) Pliable substance made by bees in their hives, 25; 2) Similar substance found in the ears.

Weasel, 53

Web: 1) Silken net spun by spider to trap insects, 19, 20; 2) Skin joining toes of some water animals and birds, 39, 41, 43, 47

Wheat, 8

Whelk, 18

Whiskers: Long, bristly hairs near the mouth.

Wings: Extensions on the bodies of birds, bats, and insects, used for flying.

Winter: The season of the year between fall and spring.

Wolf (plural, wolves), 53, 55

Wood: The tough material that makes up the trunk and branches of a tree.

Woods: A lot of trees growing together.

Worm, marine, 17

Wrasse, 30

Wriggler: Larva of mosquito, 24

Wrist: The joint where hand and arm come together.

Y

Yak, 52, 56

Z

Zebra, 52, 56

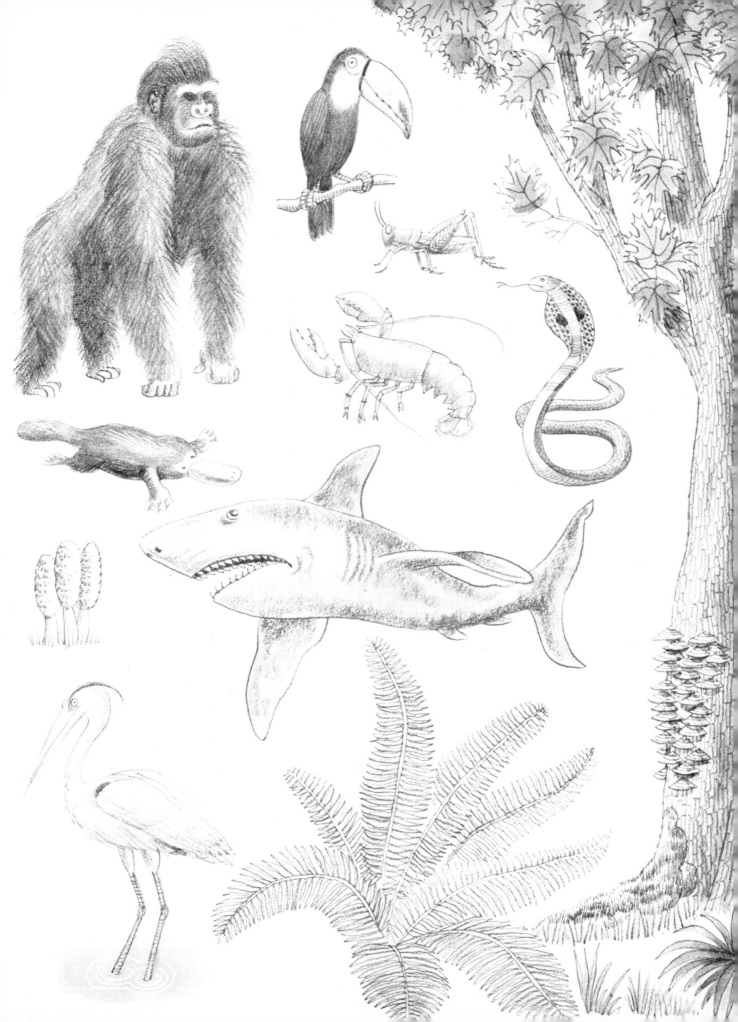